The Journey

The Journey

Poems

ANNA CATES

RESOURCE *Publications* • Eugene, Oregon

THE JOURNEY
Poems

Copyright © 2020 Anna Cates. All rights reserved. Except for brief quotations in critical publications or reviews, no part of this book may be reproduced in any manner without prior written permission from the publisher. Write: Permissions, Wipf and Stock Publishers, 199 W. 8th Ave., Suite 3, Eugene, OR 97401.

Resource Publications
An Imprint of Wipf and Stock Publishers
199 W. 8th Ave., Suite 3
Eugene, OR 97401

www.wipfandstock.com

PAPERBACK ISBN: 978-1-7252-5991-1
HARDCOVER ISBN: 978-1-7252-5989-8
EBOOK ISBN: 978-1-7252-5990-4

Manufactured in the U.S.A.   02/21/20

For Freddie, Fifi, & "Tom Cat"

God is the perfect poet.
—Robert Browning

Contents

Acknowledgements   xi
Introduction   xiii

The Book of the Dead

Venus Of Willendorf	2
Atlantis	3
Aclla	4
Pi	6
After	8
Chicken Bingo	9
Gods & Fate	11
Love & Myth	12
Time & Being	13
In Primeval Forests Deities Grew . . .	14
The Trial Of Mithras	15
Roman Holiday	16
They Did Not Dance, Nor Did They Sing	17
Invocation Of The Gods	18
The Unattached	19
Vignette	20
Haskalah	21
Book Of The Dead	22
Sacred World	24
The Elusive Quest	25

Contents

The Seeker … 26
Moving On … 27

In The Garden

Exegesis On Genesis … 30
The Frog Prince … 31
In The Garden … 33
Medusa … 35
Delilah … 37
Sign Of Jonah … 38
Martyrdom … 39
Smug Glee … 40
Alternative News … 41
Stranger … 42
A Literary Pilgrim's Progress … 43
"Just Married" … 44
Of Oaks And Bullets … 45
Question … 46
John … 47

The Nature Of The Beast

The Golem & The Nazi … 50
Gypsy … 51
Death Marches … 52
Good Friday … 53
Scrawlings After A Dream … 54
The Nature Of The Beast … 55
Rapunzel … 56

Only The Wicked

The Journey … 62
Pilgrim … 63
The Unveiling … 64
Pandora's Box … 65

Masquerade	66
Pedestal	67
Jehu Island	68
Here There Be Dragons	69
Protoge	70
On Pony Girls And Gargoyles	71
Only The Wicked (A Rondeau)	72
Confession	73
Rag Doll (A Villanelle)	74
The Naked Onion	75
Behold The Wizard	76
Father	77
Status Quo	78
Somber Musings	79
Flight	80
The Happy Guy	81
The Measure	82
When I Awake	83

Where The Butterfly Roams

The Apocalypse	86
The Second Coming	88
The Eschatologist	90
The End	91
Tundra	92
The Empty Urn	93
Never Die	94
Twilight Serenity	95
The Weed-Filled Path	96
Epilogue	97
Tau	98
Where The Butterfly Roams	99
Bibliography	101

Acknowledgements

Many thanks to the editors of the publications in which these poems first appeared:
    Scryptic: "The Apocalypse," "The Frog Prince," "Tundra," "Never Die," "Where the Butterfly Roams," "Confession," "Jehu Island"
    Angry Old Man: "Pi"
    Voice of Eve: "Masquerade," "Medusa," "The Naked Onion," "Only the Wicked," "Ragdoll," "Pandora's Box" (and a similar poem in *Eucalypt*)
    Soft Cartel: "Rapunzel"
    Anti-Heroin Chic: "Pedestal"
    The Disappointed Housewife: "Sign of Jonah"
    Otoliths: "Atlantis," "On Pony Girls & Gargoyles," "The Seeker," "The Elusive Quest," "After," "Exegesis on Genesis," "Smug Glee"
    Mock Turtle: "The Weed-Filled Path," "The Journey"
    Sheila-Na-Gig: "Venus of Willendorf"
    Immanence: "Aclla"
    Ibbetson Street: "The Measure"
    Moon: "The Empty Urn," "The Eschatologist"
    Bamboo Hut (a similar poem): "The Unveiling"
    Al-Khemia Poetica: "In the Garden"
    Blueline: "Epilogue"
    Bleached Butterfly: "Book of the Dead," "Scrawlings after a Dream," "Protégé"
    Quail Bell: "When I Awake"
    The Other Bunny: "Here There Be Dragons," "The Golem & the Nazi," "Behold the Wizard" "Moving On," "Time & Being"

Acknowledgements

Ephemerae: "They Did Not Dance, Nor Did They Sing," "Good Friday"

Contemporary Haibun Online: "Father," "The Trial of Mithras"

Cattails: "Just Married," "A Literary Pilgrim's Progress," "John," "Haskalah" (first place winner in the 2017 the *Cattails* UHTS Contest)

My Haiku Pond: Luca's Lily Pad: "twilight serenity . . . ," "Of Oaks and Bullets"

Scifaikuest: "Delilah"

Illumen: "Chicken Bingo," "Tau," "Pilgrim," "The End," "Invocation of the Gods"

Frogpond: "Roman Holiday"

Shamrock: "The Unattached," "Gods & Fate," "Sacred World"

Vita Brevis: "Love & Myth"

Kyso Flash & Accidents of Light: Kyso Flash Anthology 2018: "The Nature of the Beast"

First Literary Review-East: "Gypsy"

Atlas Poetica: "Stranger"

Haibun Today: "Status Quo," "Vignette," "In Primeval Forests Deities Grew," "Flight"

Failed Haiku: "Alternative News"

Haiku Commentary: "The Happy Guy"

Open: Journal of Arts & Letters: "Boy," "Question"

Under the Basho: "Martyrdom," "Somber Musings"

Ribbons (and similar poems in *Indian Kukai* & *Kokako*): "Death Marches"

Codex: "The Second Coming"

Introduction

In the following collection of previously published poems, I have aimed to explore the theme of religion, using a variety of poetic forms, from Japanese haibun to prose poems, from triolets to experimental free verse.

The idea for this collection began when I pulled a world religions textbook off my bookshelf and challenged myself to write at least one poem for each chapter of the book. I hope you enjoy and find meaning in the collection, though only God is a "perfect poet."

THE BOOK OF THE DEAD

VENUS OF WILLENDORF

taste your finger
then test the wind
it is not an empty bowl
beneath famished lips
but berry harvests
and venison

amid summer bloom
an artisan fashions
his diva figurine
chisels and rounds limestone
into full moon form
predating the wheel

cornucopia spills
blessings of the breast
and womb
menstrual blood flows
or the belly widens as it will
fertile fields rarely rest fallow
good boons swell
what blessings bestow

ATLANTIS

Masonic lodge—
the compass measuring
shifting zodiac

megalithic rock
erections masterminded
by megalomaniacs

elongated skulls—
mysteries of Stone Age
pyramids

September sun
sinking beneath the waves
to lost Atlantis

ACLLA

still, in desolate places
songs carry on the wind—
Capac cocha
for which there is no translation

midnight glows
through a stone window
washed with rain
as the breath
of some unspeakable beast
fogs the darkness—
Capac hucha
for which there is no translation

the beast's eyes enlarge
until it becomes a fire breathing god
demanding appeasement

ostentiferous deity fringed with snakes
promising abundant
tubers, yucca, corn

or a god of sea foam
frothing fatly into Viracocha
male and female
thriving along the pyramids' edge

screams fill the open grave
before the villagers hurl down the aclla
earthen musk fills her braided hair
as they bury her alive

the lake's silence remains unbroken
the rain learns its place
and the moths grow pale

her memory becomes
the beautiful nothingness
of a vanished people
testifying to how everything once known
can so easily become forgotten[1]

---

1. Parrinder, *World Religions*, 90–100.

PI

capital pi
small alpha
capital omega
electron dot structures
& radius squared = 3.14
the question of epsilon (0.007)
and other constants of the universe
but can saying make it so?

dualistic world views
laden with male/female binaries
envisioned ancient & younger deities
within each culture, color & space correlations:

Time/gods:	North	East	South	West
Chichimecs	white	green	red	yellow
Toltecs	red	yellow	white	green
Maya	white	red	yellow	black
Aztecs	black	yellow	blue	white

13 #s in tonalamatl + 20 day-signs = good
13 = good; 4 bad
(20) 13-day time periods = 1 cardinal space point & parallel god
+ the xiuhpoalli:
(18) 20-day periods & parallel gods
ritualized time-units
the Aztec tonalpoalli
spiraling from the evolving universe
day names, festivals, & solar years:
2-Acatl to 1-Tochtli
alpha and omega
the beginning and the end

days signs & parallel gods:
1 Imix & parallel gods
2 Ik & parallel gods
3 Akbal & parallel gods
4 Kan & parallel gods
5 Chicchan & parallel gods
6 Cimi & parallel gods
7 Manik & parallel gods
8 Lamat & parallel gods
9 Muluc & parallel gods
10 Oc & parallel gods
11 Chuen and parallel gods
12 Eb & parallel gods
13 Ben & parallel gods
14 (1) Ix & parallel gods
15 (2) Men & parallel gods
16 (3) Cib & parallel gods
17 (4) Caban & parallel gods
18 (5) Eznab & parallel gods
19 (6) Cauac & parallel gods
20 (7) Ahau & parallel gods . . .

and so we exit Aztlan
the journey sacred onus
as the psalter sang:
each soul holds some certitude
but only for a moment
the blossoms of bliss[2]

---

2. Parrinder, *World Religions*, 69–89.

AFTER

Marduk slew the monster Tiamat, Shamash rose like the sun between mountains, grasping his rod of justice. Ishtar made love and war, beside the Tree of Life, beyond the marsh reed village, where rose the first ziggurat—Butchers, bakers, tradesmen, herdsmen, field hands, artisans, guards, storekeepers, slaves, eunuchs, prostitutes, scribes, priests and priestesses gifted to the gods: barley, dates, onions, fish, fruit, fowl, milk, honey, ghee. Divination discerned divine will—Read for omens: lungs and livers, horrific births, speech, gait, moles, animal or bird movements. Horoscopes. Astrology. Oily patterns on water told all, comprised omen text, exorcist's or doctor's prognosis, law and order, truth and justice . . .[3]

libations
poured out for the dead
incense acrid and sweet

---

3. Parrinder, *World Religions*, 114–134.

CHICKEN BINGO

Big debate
play chicken bingo
or tango with the champs
with the odds of fungi . . .

Ten thousand miles up only blue nucleus
Kiddush blessing and wine for blood
clocks work backwards and donkeys
pull wagons through memory
down red dust covered streets
while spring works whole multitudes
into welters of vernalagnia

Down below
mud and oppression
dirty bombs exploding
while every time piece wastes the hours
men cup bruised balls
and female complaints remain censored
forget Babylonian devils
and the jackals haunting deserts
where is the Supreme Being
rising like the sun between mountains
grasping his rod of justice?

Villagers read for omens
lungs and livers
oily patterns on water
bones

As simple as *if x then y*—
kittum u mesharum—

The entrails
of a chicken—
bingo![4]

---

4. Parrinder, *World Religions*, 135–145.

GODS & FATE

The Golden Ass—
Hecate waits
at the crossroads

In the days of old, city states devoted themselves to the moon goddess. Snakes entwined her sinewy arms, while the wood nymph hugged her sacred tree. Shady consorts encircled Zeus with his definitive thunderbolt.

Constellations guided sojourners across rough seas. Chalices filled to bacchanalian levels; cornucopia, lubricity, garlic wreaths, agape, and the wings of victory. And thus, the villagers danced with goat-footed Pan, centaurs, and satyrs. Hermaphrodites donned laurel leaves. Sacred bees swirled from hyperborean sunshine into crazy starlight.

Oedipus pondered the unknowable future, the will of the gods, a world where kings, queens, and paupers strut and fret through divine drama. No mythology, the truth he beheld at his blindness.[5]

distant thunder—
pausing in the shadow
of the Sphinx

---

5. Parrinder, *World Religions*, 146–161.

LOVE & MYTH

Before the Maori venerated Io, Maui pulled up from the sea land dripping in seashells, forging islands, stealing fire from the underworld. He ate the flames like the high priest's morsel from his servant's instrument . . .

The priest is untouched. The tapu is unbroken. The fire ever burns.[6]

tropical bird calls
the last mango falls
Hawaiian twilight
at a sunset hula
the final aloha

---

6. Parrinder, *World Religions*, 49–59.

TIME & BEING

In Tibetan Buddhism, sufferers of bad and good karma alike succumb to three cardinal sins, incur six spheres of existence, experience the chain of causation, and death holds together the Wheel of Life . . .[7]

I The cock (passion)
August air
full of feathers . . .
pecking order

II The serpent (hatred)
dusky pines . . .
where campfire flickers
a rat snake's forked tongue

III The pig (stupidity)
summer haze . . .
along with some comrades
a pot-bellied sow

---

7. Parrinder, *World Religions*, 262–303.

IN PRIMEVAL FORESTS DEITIES GREW...

Dravidian jungle nomads chanted praise to lords of thunder and rain. *Gonds* gifted deities with worshipful acts. Guardian clans sacrificed sheep, goats. Iron spear points and yak tail fly-whisks punctuated Hindu temple worship. *Ifugao* gods filled five regions of universe; when threatened with cholera or smallpox, devotees bowed to the sky.[8]

blooming lotus
a child follows a cow
to the riverbank

8. Parrinder, *World Religions*, 35–48.

THE TRIAL OF MITHRAS

salt desert
a scientist's Mazda purrs
to a halt

In the beginning, the evil one ruptured the sky's rampart, bringing havoc, death, and pain . . .

Persia. The fire ritual fire began. The communion meal commenced. Magi arrived with gifts, barsom twigs, and handshakes. Sacrificial bull . . .[9]

blue mountains
the soul thirsty
as the Gobi

---

9. Parrinder, *World Religions*, 177–191.

ROMAN HOLIDAY

Arab junkyard—
stray dogs and baboons comb
moonlit rubbish

Today, such unlikely relationships mystify scientists. But 2,000 years before Copernicus the question was, *Vaticanus*? And, *What veracity in blue Venus veiled in haze*?

In ancient Rome, Republicans pondered how a virgin might best devote herself to Vesta. Drinking molten metal became the penalty for breaking solemn vow. Augustine condemned such political religion as opium.

The *Golden Ass* teamed with magic—the evil eye, numina in menstrual blood and iron, magic circles, odd numbers, lunar powers, protective spitting, and sex changes. Republicans donned their magical amulets to ward off disease and chanted, *Be gone vile demon hydrophobia*!

Near the Villa of Mysteries, initiation, flagellation, mystical phallus and the promise of eternal bliss.[10]

---

10. Parrinder, *World Religions*, 162–176.

THEY DID NOT DANCE, NOR DID THEY SING

"Wisdom is the distance plotted between two points on a continuum," the Sadducee said.

A Pharisee shook his head. "No, it is the continuum itself."

A Zealot rolled his eyes with a huff. "The continuum is something else entirely!"

A young boy laughed. They turned toward the wall where he sat. The sun beat down, and the silence shriveled them.

a peddler
with olives and figs—
holy land

INVOCATION OF THE GODS

Ancestral shrine—
Beneath a liquid moon,
a girl lights a candle,
recalling the ti of dead kings,
the manna of all departed.

Cinnamon, wine, and precious stones—
Oxen, sheep, and oracle bones—
The ceremonial jade disc
limbers up for magic ritual,
and the dragon rides the thunder.

Warm rain—
The lotus soaks in the ecstasy.
A priestess arrives, washed and scented.
She dances as flutes and pap-pipes blow,
as zithers strum and bells chime.
She dips and spins like a dove in the sky,
decked in a red silk dress,
a courtship ritual to invoke the gods
to descend for erotic union.[11]

---

11. Parrinder, *World Religions*, 304–352.

THE UNATTACHED

A leaf of grass
In bondage to the wind—
Karma

Ask a linguist or Jain, literary critic or philosopher, to solve the puzzle of this heterodoxy. Speech cannot describe reality without contradiction. Qualified speech is corollary to the doctrine of maybe. Syad-vada.

X is infinite denies impermanence. *Maybe x is infinite* is more correct, acknowledges other possibilities: Maybe no, maybe yes, maybe both.

Souls suffer limitation, expansion, contraction, transmigration—are classified into five categories:

Touch: Sunlight opens the tea leaf.
Taste: Blood seduces the flea.
Smell: Wildflowers draw the bee.
Sight: My fluffy cat delights me.
Sound: Its purring soothes me.

Yes, no, or maybe . . .[12]

---

12. Parrinder, *World Religions*, 241–249.

VIGNETTE

bansuri tune
a boy lights a swastika
of candles

By the River Ravi, near the village of Kartarpur, a yogi sits cross-legged in the dust. At the Golden Temple, pilgrims proffer coins for bread. By the sacred waters, songs lure Sikh bathers. Across the Pool of Nectar, beside the gatehouse, before the throne of the timeless god, the tireless sunset...[13]

blood rain
the solemn eyes
of a hijra

---

13. Parrinder, *World Religions*, 250–261.

HASKALAH

Beyond organic culture, neo-platonic ideas, post Hasmonean Kabbalah in Ashkenazi ritual, and dogmatic assertions . . .

phylacteries—
beneath a prayer shawl
epiphany

After mystical aspirations, codes in the Torah, homiletical instruction, and Hasidic communion . . . Celestial palaces and chariots. Cosmological tetragrammation . . .

Wailing Wall—
a rabbi's head bobs
pilgrimage and tears

Share the cup of wine. Let the ram's fat sizzle. After Babylonian origins and orgiastic elements; barley harvests and Passover festivals, a new advent . . .[14]

ram's horn—
a Chanukah candle
erupts in flame

---

14. Parrinder, *World Religions*, 385–419.

BOOK OF THE DEAD

Inferred confessions
sinners with constellations tangled in their hair
fragility, ghosts, skeletons escaped from closets
and moored at the docks like Charon
ferryman to Hell
complaints of no pulse
bottomless underworlds
unfinished phone calls . . .

Bobby _____ stands apart with his fly down
confounded and caught in the rain
like Spiderman snared by a web of his own design
or Superman with kryptonite
he's lost his 3D glasses and seems unable to talk
can't even squawk unlike the ravens
brooding along the power lines above him

Miley Cyrus joined the Luciferian Illuminati
the prophet tells him
her name-change in honor of Osiris
Egyptian god of the dead
Bobby swoons from the Egyptology
as the Mormon missionaries exit the property

Bobby _____ recalls that book he checked out
from the library long ago and finds himself
another beastie, lost in sarcophagi bitumen
with jackals and bulls, composite amalgams,
river valley creeds and cosmologies, Serapis cults,
sun worship, and Heliopolitan pattern triads,
converging in liturgical papyrus spells,

Ptolemaic Age hymns to gods, charcoal and incense,
sacred banquet beneath the great Eye of Horus,
Cheops, Chephren, Micerinus, scarabs, obelisks,
Apis, Anubis, ithyphallic Min as the sun rides
the celestial bull's horns till daylight ends
and the sun god journeys through underworld again,
hieroglyphic ritual mythology with the earth rising
from a lotus blossom in primordial waters, artisan,
bisexual deities, erotic unions, adze against the lips,
brain exhumed, intestines excavated, sexual organs
eviscerated for fragrant spices, natron and oil,
the heart heavy with the halls of Hell[15]

---

15. Parrinder, *World Religions*, 135–145.

SACRED WORLD

Don't spend a lifetime in blindness. On parallel paths bells perfume spring air with rhythm. Apocrypha blooms rhyme in aster-like asterisks. Twined in the fingers of a serpent handler, the great snake Wollonqua* quivers.

So embrace the everlasting. All truth is God's truth. The Djanggawul Sisters birthed the Aborigines in Dreamtime**. To each his own *tjurunga*** beneath the revered *rangga*****.

gum leaf song
a taste of witchety grubs
and berries

*An Aboriginal mythological snake
**An Aboriginal myth
***Sacred emblem
****Ceremonial pole[16]

THE ELUSIVE QUEST

Night falls over Africa. Ezekiel's wheel whorls in circles. The city swallows in electric light Jacob's ladder, stairway to the stars . . .

Behind the dark curtain, an ancient past, when Mother Earth, Ala, dodged Shango's thunderbolts, and Olokun, the sea god, rose from the Atlantic on mudfish legs, in each hand a grand lizard . . .

Today, the Rozi still dance, and masked forms still celebrate the dead.[17]

sojourn . . .
pushing forward
on mudfish legs

---

17. Parrinder, *World Religions*, 60–68.

THE SEEKER

... faith is a phenomenological construct nagging parasitic conviction paradise retains capital importance maranatha doctrine recreates re-imagined moksha nirvana we posit speculative interrelations parables and representations re-interpreting them leads to the gods perishing heaven or hell animal mineral or vegetable the weal and woe reincarnation to transubstantiation we ponder an inescapable fate soul travel and stars so inexplicable so vast ... [18]

a candle burns
in a dark window
frozen starlight

---

[18]. Parrinder, *World Religions*, 192–240.

MOVING ON

prayer beads
falling apart—
henna designs

Sunset and sand. Near the well of Zam-Zam, outside the Kaaba, dusty pilgrims end their sojourn.

We share a common humanity. As kings have reached out to grasp the Kaaba's black stone, we too reach out, twirl like dervishes, or squat on prayer rugs, coiled up like spiders with our *kabair* (big sins) or *saghair* (little sins), not wanting, really, to throw stones, only enjoy the magic carpet ride.

Though arches hold up *kalam* (theology), skulking beneath gold domes, we feel so cold, dirty with petrodollars, questioning Ali's metempsychosis or what-not, wondering if we might, or might not, be blessed.[19]

prayer call—
a camel shakes his head
and walks on

---

19. Parrinder, *World Religions*, 462–507.

IN THE GARDEN

EXEGESIS ON GENESIS

Details tell stories, curate time, how latitude and longitude eased from formlessness into new world order—the promise, the land, perhaps some purple-skied parallel reality where retrospection haunts what steps off the beaten path—the animal within—but with chocolate and daisies who's afraid of Virginia Wolf? Fictions rework logos, create time-warps

to wastelands or paradisal plains—voice or void—mountains converge into new mythologies before red eyes, before the hypnotized . . . exegesis on Genesis.

a philosopher
sighs in a stick-built house
winter wind

THE FROG PRINCE

he stepped from the bog
and stood before her naked
hair topped with algae
skin cerulean as death
scented of frog
I am Adam
I am clay

she dropped the gothic romance
voiceless as Eve
aghast at what she'd bitten into
and quaked
but if I die before I wake . . .

chill his webbed fingers yet colder his kiss
but it was she who felt frozen
till words filled her mouth
as the knowledge summered in her soul
you're the man who disappeared last year
they searched for you, but . . .

he hushed her with a grin
every tree has its shadow; I my rib
I've waited for you, watched a thousand times
come be my night swan
come float on the water with me

she took his hand
she tossed her sandals
she stepped toward the bank
her feet sank into the muck
and the water enveloped her

IN THE GARDEN

Ohio August
mild from El Nino
the sun broods like a neighbor over
Rolling Terrace Trailer Park Home
you taste the dust
from the pot-holed pavement
as you pace the garden
like the Georgian peasant
in her gypsy kerchief
tending the cabbage patch
beside the communal farm
antique tractors riding adamic sod
in camaraderie for MotherCountry
like the picture book of communist Russia
I checked out from the Paris
Public Library—when was it—1988?

The primordial garden welcomes us back
tomatoes sag on the vines
sunflowers droop like withered breasts
shading burgeoning beans
we trespass into okra
hovering above the mint leaves
scenting the breeze
beside the Rose of Sharon
and broken corn stocks
bereft of any scarecrow

The primeval archetype envelops us
we sink forward with the tomatoes
amazed to behold such weeds
we dry out and bend like the sunflowers
having no other recourse
but to bow low

MEDUSA*

Beware, my pretty ones,
the green-eyed monster, Jealousy.
As bards have sung, she mocks
the meat she feasts upon—
Though cuckolds live in bliss,
Hell hath no fury like a woman scorned.

Athena breathed life into that adage,
like Elohim, fashioning Adam from clay,
like Anunnaki forming his golem,
and thus, forged the Gorgon,
twin to her inner demon, Jealousy.

Mad women battle voices in their heads,
but Medusa heard only hissing,
silken tresses raging into snakes—
No matter that she'd been raped—
Like a snail, she slunk away,
retreating into herself, abjuring human
company, abiding in ruins on Sarpedon,
forgetting forever the pleasant ring
of friendly chatter, haunted by screams
of men turned to stone, for, monstrous
though she was, still they came,
like waves breaking over rock,
clinging to their chimera.

Think on it, my pretties, and learn.
Say it, my pretties, and mean it:
"I care not for husbands,
only brothers and sons."

*As told by Ovid, after Poseidon raped the beautiful maiden Medusa in Athena's temple, the livid Athena turned Medusa's lovely hair into snakes and made her visage so horrible to behold that men turned to stone at the mere sight of it.

DELILAH

It wasn't the sweetness of grapes that she slipped onto his tongue, but olives soaked in brine. It wasn't love she offered, but comfort, ease after his toils, for a man as powerful as he was always sought out—he, the man with the magic hair that had never been cut—he who had yet to break his vows.

He lay back onto her lap. She toyed like a weaver with his braids, trying to read him like a blind girl with braille. He closed his eyes with a groan. He boarded the boat. Wind took the sail and carried him across the sea. He crept ashore and nestled into the shadows beneath a Dragon Tree. And his hair kept growing, growing as if it were all of him. It rooted through the soil till he became like the tree itself, trunk stiff.

He awoke to sky naked of clouds, ropes binding him, and his head cold, *cold*! And the grin on her face was without remorse.

a witch doctor
with his bag of bones . . .
dragon's blood

SIGN OF JONAH

The lady who kept her lover's
used Trojans in a shoe box,
anglers in a dirt-filled aquarium,
to feed her four hens
along with their own eggshells—
the lady with the toy poodle
always sniffing the cat's ass,
a first edition Yeats on the shelf—
dreamed she lived by the sea,
on the outskirts of some hyperborean
domain, dusky forests deep with pine.
Outside the French patio doors,
puffins paced along the rocks,
till darkness descended like a shroud,
and Christ returned, ruffling feathers,
turning rock to bread, sea to blood,
the clouds bright. And she writhed
like the earthworms, clucked at the fowl,
understood dogs will be dogs,
sensed some luck in the Atlantic gales.
And the sky rolled back like a scroll . . .

MARTYRDOM

In the fifth grade, I first heard that the end of the world could be nigh. I needed to watch for the "signs of the times." But the whole idea of the world going through such a terrible ordeal, the "Tribulation," horrified me. I dreamed about it. I was arrested. I was led up the wooden steps to the guillotine. To my surprise, nothing happened. For no reason I can explain, nobody beheaded me.

"I'm so disappointed in you," my mother told me in the dream, her countenance a sour frown. She took it as a spiritual failure on my part that I wouldn't be promptly executed.

an Egyptologist
with scarabs in her eyes
camel moon

SMUG GLEE

Years ago, at the Foursquare Gospel Church, I was surprised when the guest preacher lunged out at me, remonstrating about how glad I should feel to live in America. I just don't see how I had that coming. I was just sitting there, pat on the pew, like everyone else. Was I not "plastic smile club" enough?

church picnic
speaking in tongues
a mocking jay

ALTERNATIVE NEWS

Florida, an evangelical church announces a new ministry:
washing the feet of prostitutes . . .

April rain
an earthworm
searching too

STRANGER

Diving through Utah, along lonely highway, I pull into a rest stop. A man asks me, "Do you wear special underwear?"

red rock
tumbleweeds roll
the cloudless sky
in a dry land
Mormon temples

A LITERARY PILGRIM'S PROGRESS

In 1992 I took a "junior's abroad" class trip to study "The British Literary Landscape." We visited Shakespeare's Stratford-on-Avon and Wordsworth's lake district. In Canterbury, the acerbic evangelical history professor warned us, "Don't venture inside the New Age boutiques. This is no longer a place for Christian pilgrims." But I wasn't afraid of dangling crystals and ceramic dragons . . .

cultish boutique
a pyramid shimmers
in rainbow sunlight

"JUST MARRIED"

After attending a community ice cream social, I drop by Dollar Tree to buy green tea. On the way home, an Amish-style buggy slows me down. Now, I know Ohio has overtaken Pennsylvania in numbers of Amish, but I hadn't noticed any settling near my hometown of Wilmington. I draw closer to the carriage. Peacock feathers cover it, and it sports a "Just Married" sign. A passing glimpse of bride and groom: both men in clean white shirts. "Gee," I say to myself in feigned ignorance, "Maybe they're Quakers."

June dusk
a horse whip lashing
full honey moon

OF OAKS AND BULLETS

missives—
the sanctuary
so empty

Two soldiers. Each hides behind a tree. Each holds a gun. Each harbors the same objective: Kill or be killed.

wasted moon—
the world feels colder
alone

QUESTION

desert sky opening a purgatory of rain . . .

A mystery: Who to blame for the man buried up to his neck in the ground, eyelids cut off, head covered in honey to attract stinging fire ants?

I heard Indians were to blame, then, no, Spaniards.

And who was that goddamn man anyway?

cactus bloom fall
the light and darkness
in a stranger's eyes

JOHN

He dreamed of being devoured by pigs, from seriously fat squashers to girls simply greedy for him, porcine noses snorting as they fought to get enough of him, a task at which he hoped they'd never fully succeed.

3:16
scrawled in the sand
the tide takes it all

THE NATURE OF THE BEAST

THE GOLEM & THE NAZI

Genesis, dusk . . .

With the sweet crunch still fresh in his mouth, Adam perceives a change. A cool breeze causes him to shudder. He sees traces of dirt packed into the cracks of his palm and feels like a golem, clay brought to life, raw form kneaded as bread into a shapely husk, and yet, forever dust, coming from dust and to dust returning . . .

After cryptology . . .

Anunnaki writes the *shem*, a name for God, on a scrap of papyrus and inserts the honied text into the golem's mouth. Like Pinocchio coming to life, the golem speaks, "Aye," turning into a man, almost. Then Anunnaki writes *emet*, truth, on his forehead, so he'll never tell a lie and warns him, "I can cut the aleph from your inscription, creature, changing it from truth to death, *emet* to *met*." But the golem only stares back with his sunken eyes, illiterate, uncomprehending . . .

WWII . . .

The Nazi scales the synagogue stairs, determined to find the golem, forged from clay from the Vltava River bank then awakened through rabbinical ritual—a golem who can raise the dead and become invisible. *A bolshevist's puppet*, the Nazi thinks, teeth clenched, *a demonic fiend who challenges the swastika, a murderous rapist who lost at love, hidden in the synagogue attic* (a place no Nazi should trod alone).

He opens the door. He scans the darkness. He raises his knife, careful on his shiny black jackboots. When the golem springs from the shadows, monstrous as a gargoyle, the Nazi slashes at the inscription, scratching off the *aleph*, changing *emet* to *met*, truth to death. The Nazi turns to ash in the synagogue's burning, but the golem escapes into the night, the crystalline, starry, starry night.[20]

blood moon
what a single spark
will do

---

20. "Golem." https://en.wikipedia.org/wiki/Golem

GYPSY

She saw the end before it happened, like the ancients reading bones. Mercurial hazel eyes glimpsed it, glinting in the sea green beryl stone. She divined it through tarot, heard it in a midnight owl, felt it in Black Forest nettles, though more so in a villager's scowl. She tasted it in mandrake's sweet sting. Images in the sea green beryl stone.

Omens tingled through her, mystical powers of the moon, stirring her like the tides. Yet what could she do? Her foresight sickened her till she refused to believe—what the wind makes moan—It simply couldn't be. Silver skulls dancing, shining, laughing. Bodies burning in the sea green beryl stone.

a silver spoon
to measure the sea—
lamentations

DEATH MARCHES

Today no flags flap, no troops contend, no dead cows fill fields, adding their wasted meat to the corpses. Drums recede into history. Just a light wind tosses the canopy of leaves. And yet, the heaviness in my heart . . .

Nazi ruins
where inmates trod the extra mile
lily of the valley

GOOD FRIDAY

It doesn't take a Halloween costume to rule the world. Today, leaning out the window of her red brick home, a widow tends the petunias in her flower box . . .

flag country—
swastika tattoo
and stubble

SCRAWLINGS AFTER A DREAM

You stood beside that dark door
Where they herded the women like cattle.
They entered one by one, "bitch" to "whore."
You stayed outside that dark door.
To each his own; I've heard the adage before.
But why should people be treated as chattel?
You stood beside that dark door
Where they herded the women like cattle.

THE NATURE OF THE BEAST

My freshman year in college, in Psychology 101, our professor prompted us to debate the question: Is humanity basically good or basically evil? Today, I'm still not sure I have the answer.

holocaust museum—
the emptiness filling
display case shoes

RAPUNZEL

I

Her hair wasn't really golden, but more of a strawberry blond. Yet that wasn't the point. What mattered was its length. She'd grown her hair unusually long, so long that the ends became antennae, attracting cosmic energies, or so Himmler supposed, the former chicken farmer who'd gone from feathers to Nazi frills. If he could harness the ancient Aryan occult powers, like Wodin and Thor, purge himself of Lemurian animalism, that would be a good start toward racial restoration. Then he'd wield the thunderbolt, mighty as a god, sealing his fate to be Germany's next fuhrer.

"Take her into 'protective custody,'" he told his SS officers. And so, they locked her in a Wewelsburg Castle tower.

II

"Your racial science teacher says you draw pictures of your oracular visions," Himmler drilled her the following day, seated behind his desk, strewn with papers.

She shrugged. "Mutter says I'm a habitual doodler." She laughed weakly, seated in the chair on the other side of his desk.

Himmler leaned forward. "Do you play tarot? What spells or charms do you know? Do you need special herbs, mandrake, a sparrow to cut up? Do you know where to find the Spear of Destiny?"

"I'm Lutheran. I must just have the gift of prophecy. That's all. A gift from God. I can't force it. I've never dabbled in the darker side."

Himmler smirked, glad the Christian veneer would soon be washed away from Germany forever. At least she wasn't a Jehovah's Witness. He peered again at the picture she'd scrawled just prior to her graduation, a picture portraying, or so she claimed, a scene from the future: A big white rocket with a red "USA," the details uncanny, though different from the V-2, alongside a sketch of a middle-aged man that most women would consider tolerable to look at. A paternalistic grin on the eerily familiar face. Himmler's heart sped with excitement when he realized who it was, albeit seasoned by a few more years: *Von Braun, that moon-crazed dreamer!*

"Ever been to Peenumunde, Rapunzel?" he punned.

"Never. Why do you ask?"

He raised his brows. "We're presently at war with the U.S., my dear. You suggest one of our top physicists would collaborate with our enemies in such a grand, cosmic scheme?"

She huffed, rolling her eyes. "I've only drawn what I saw, Herr Himmler, just as you bid. I didn't know who the man was, but his image flickered into my mind with the sky rocket. When can I go home?" she finished in a mouse-like squeak.

"Draw more scenes from the future. I'll get you all the art supplies you need. For now, you're dismissed."

Once they'd ushered her back down the hall, Himmler called one SS officer back. "No scissors, no knife, no razor, nothing sharp is to be brought to her room." The cadet, unable to conceal his grin, clicked his heels together. "Heil Hitler!"

III

Days later, she slipped the next illustration onto Himmler's desk. He scanned the page, stoic.

"Hoodlums, tearing down a wall."

She nodded.

"What does it mean?"

"The fall of bolshevism."

"When?"

She closed her eyes. "I'm thinking 1989 or thereabouts."

His head jut forward. "That's a *long* time away!"

"The *final* fall."

He nodded with a grin. "Your prophetic powers fascinate me, fraulein. Yet they could be better directed, expanded."

"Just what do you mean to say, Herr Himmler?"

"Appreciating their origin would be a start. Then you might learn to draw up horoscopes, engage in a few rituals, seances, and so forth. We'll make a good pagan out of you yet."

"And if I'm not interested?"

His smile wavered. "It's all for the glory of the Reich. How can you consider refusing?" He shook his head with a sigh. That she would be so cheeky! "You know I like you, fraulein. You shouldn't think to test me. I wouldn't want to have to do something drastic. Consider your family."

She shuddered, the oldest of eight. "But if I anger God, he'll take my gift away. Or worse! Surely, you understand my reluctance to offend him."

To her surprise, he shook his head. "No, fraulein, I cannot." He leaned forward. "I cannot imagine the silly female fancies swirling through your head." His fist fell onto the ledger, rattling writing instruments and causing her to flinch. "There is no god in the sky as you imagine! The only gods are earthly spirits. We can commune with them, the pagan gods of our ancestors, Wodin and Thor."

But that's blasphemy, idolatry, she wanted to say then thought better of it. Obviously, he didn't care. *Children, kitchen, and church*—the ideal lifestyle for the German woman—but not *too* churchy it would seem.

"May I go now?"

"See what else you can envision." He twirled his fingers through the air dismissively, turning away to reach for his phone.

She rose from her seat. "Sieg heil," she whispered, lifting a limp limb.

IV

That night, a summer solstice celebration ensued. In mystical reverie, cadets lit bon fires and jumped over the flames, taking care not to burn themselves. Liquor bottles clinked under the starlight, cigarette smoke swirling through the air. Officers loitered with red-lipped ostarbeiters, slave girls harvested from the east, with round heads and empty eyes, Poles perhaps, or Russians. Herr Himmler, rider's crop in hand, laughed uproariously at her and the other two clairvoyants as they—naked and on their hands and knees—pushed marbles across the floor with their noses, racing toward the middle of the swastika, long braids snaking along the dusty floor beside them.

V

Two days passed. Another sketch in hand, she stepped inside Himmler's office, averting her gaze. She sat in the empty seat then reluctantly handed him the paper. His eyes riveted onto the artwork. Then he peered up. "Two smoking skyscrapers, fraulein?"

She squirmed on her sore ass. "Future terrorism in the west."

Himmler stiffened. "I was expecting something else. I know you can't force these things, fraulein, but you could at least try to get this god, or devil, or whatever opens your mind, to show you the Reich's glorious destiny." He leaned forward. "How about wonder weapons? Astonishing inventions like Die Glocke I told you about? What more can Germany do to hasten our world domination? Dazzle me with your psychic powers!"

She groaned, shoulders slumped. "I'll try to discern what you want me to foretell, but I can't make any promises."

VI

That afternoon, alone in her room, she drifted into a deep sleep then awoke with a jerk, covered in sweat. A new image flickered through her mind. She grabbed her pad of paper and began to pencil it out: Smoke from forest fires engulfing alien skyscrapers, endless miles of dry cracked earth, fuming with heat. Germany in the clutches of global warming. She crumpled up the paper. *That's not what Herr Himmler wants to see. That's not what I want to see*! She threw her pad and pencil across the room. A train whistled in the distance, heralding some mysterious doom. She cupped the sides of her head. Advancing armies. Exploding bombs. Starving slaves in rags. She fell to her knees, hands balled together. "Oh, merciful God in Heaven, let not this terrible end come to be!"

VII

A week passed. Blond fuzz grew at the bottoms of her legs. Locked in the tower, she waited, waited for a price, a Samson with his eyes gouged out, a witch, a Rumplestiltskin, anyone who'd miraculously appear beneath her window and hasten that sordid episode of her life to an end. But only SS officers came and went, marching in their dark uniforms, silver skulls glinting.

"My hair. It's got to go," she sighed. And so, that night, with the full moon glimmering, she started pulling, wincing and pulling, till her scalp bled, and her hands ached, and her neck muscles burned, and her body shook, strawberry blond pooling in a pile beside her. She gritted her teeth and pulled, destroying her "antennae," till she was bald as a concentration camp inmate, ready for the ovens.

ONLY THE WICKED

THE JOURNEY

the path winds on
where the river runs

geese flee for winter
imagine aching wings

blind pathways to the moon
the earth moving below

the corpus yielding
to sensations of sky

silent noegenesis
bridging chasms of sea

in acts of xenization
all of us pilgrims

PILGRIM

Truth
like runes on a scroll
whose crumbling papyrus in its fragility
both holds and hides the signs
the enigmas

Love and hate
God or fate
and how and why
have we arrived at this strange place?

On either side of the mountains
tramontane winds
we might lose our way
though rivers jut through that land
like redemption

We carry on
though rain obscures the limits
we carry on . . .
. . . or tarry

THE UNVEILING

first raindrops soak into parched loam
like seeds that sink so softly into the soul
there paramount inaugurations take hold
where raindrops soak into parched loam
where woods wax wild or gardens grow
where mystery creeps with fairies or gnomes
first raindrops soak into parched loam
like seeds that sink so softly into the soul

PANDORA'S BOX

a child doesn't understand the darkness
laden with stars yet fears
patching the cracks with absence or harshness
a child doesn't understand the darkness
of black holes the enigma of emptiness
distances conjured in light years
a child doesn't understand the darkness
laden with stars yet fears

MASQUERADE

diamond chiara
feathers of red or blue

goblin
cat or bandit

she hides
cheeks and eyes

behind the mask
because she's shy

she betrays no magic
to gods of mountain or sky

she wears the mask
because she's shy

gods on the mountain
gods in the sky

she wears the mask
because she's shy

PEDESTAL

I

She always wanted to view the world
from a pedestal but couldn't climb that high.
She was poor, a nobody, another addicted girl . . .
She always wanted to view the world
from a fresh perspective, where horizons curled
into rainbow beauty, redeeming the whole sky.
She always wanted to view the world
from a pedestal but couldn't climb that high.

II

I've waited to put you on a pedestal.
But spring has ended, and the flowers have dropped their bloom.
Then summer green faded into cold wind. Lamentable,
though I've waited to put you on a pedestal,
written poems, sang songs, and told parables
like Jesus in the garden, tired and accepting a strange doom,
though I've waited to put you on a pedestal,
when spring ended, and the bleeding hearts dropped their bloom.

JEHU ISLAND

Leave your mother, Alpha.
Sail across the briny abyss.

Reclaim abandoned shores,
And pry back the bracken

To behold the uncertain truth.
Pick through the briars'

Intoxication of red rose,
And if you keep your footing

Sure, and don't slip
Like a lemming over the crags

Into the mouth of the kraken,
You will find your end, your Omega.

You will arrive full circle . . .
If . . .

HERE THERE BE DRAGONS

My eyes have turned to glass, beautiful things that can never see a full moon eclipsed by cloud like a pirate's patch that censors blindness.

A parrot squawks at me, muttering the same phrase repeatedly, a reverie about poetry, words comprising a vast sea where sail the golden gods on glistening ships—Plunders, pillages, and rapes, songs sung to cinch the irony as bull whips crack with time across backs or boards, creaking with sea-sickness, decks slippery with vomited rum.

Elsewhere silence locks like a peg leg, stuck in nocturnal quicksand—Jungle muddle livid
as God with snakes.

vine-covered cave
on a stone tablet
curious cuneiform

PROTOGE

"Some wizards choose
rainbow colors,
others light.
But beware
the deceptive glimmer
of fool's gold, my child."

"The light is greater
than the darkness . . ."
The good wizard huffs,
"It's *not* all about
dragon's glass
at the end of a staff!"

ON PONY GIRLS AND GARGOYLES

looking forward
looking back
no exits
only fresh starts

a Catholic boy
caught in the act balks
forms pearly history
glistening luminous
the city in the rain

beside graffiti
pilgrims quaff symbolic draught
while piano notes empower
the suggestion of a j walk
down metaphysical Main Street

even cold rooms
tell stories
imaginary parrots
pace and squawk

watch the pony girls and listen
to the gargoyles that talk
cleansing showers
baptize beggars by the kiosk

ONLY THE WICKED (A RONDEAU)

Only the wicked ask for a sign
Shrouded in fog by the restless brine
Like two strange birds, we overwinter
Cast stale bread into the water
And sing a strain of *Auld Lang Syne*

Fateful, when constellations align
Facades of banquet bells and blushing wine
Generations of sons and daughters
Yet only the wicked ask for a sign

Docks invade the gray borderline
Charades and simulations enshrine
Deceptive shimmer that splinters
As a result of what we slaughter
I am his sin, and he is mine
Only the wicked ask for a sign

CONFESSION

. . . And he opened his mouth to the midnight rain,
hypnotized by the star's antigodlin descent,
and worshipped it. —Anonymous

If I forget myself, don't ask why.
If my gray eyes shine a little too silver at times,
remember, you, too, could have been
the unlucky sojourner that night.

Never you mind
why I was roaming after gloaming in the wilds.
We're all entitled to a secret or two—
It could just as easily have been you
who first mistook that bat for a screech owl.

It would shock you to know the truth—
I'm not all crucifixes and prayers.
I've drunk the holy water, but to no avail.
The curse lurks within me—
As the moon turns tides,
I cycle into lunatic with unspeakable lusts.

Still, spare me your silver bullets.
It could just as easily have been you,
bitten that night in the thickets,
bristling into something new,
becoming the shadow stranger of nightmare
who'd roast your heart on a skewer—
Your parish priest, the vampire.

RAG DOLL (A VILLANELLE)

Memories moor along the burden I feel
Shrouded in the fog of that bay
And autumn chill settles into the gull's reel

Where sky and sea congeal
Portents speak in shades of gray
Memories moor along the burden I feel

A tiresome journey's big reveal
How souls shatter like jars of clay
And autumn chill settles into the gull's reel

A rag doll isn't made of steel
I'm confounded by the fray
Memories moor along the burden I feel

Our human blight the woe and the weal
Along the lonesome quay I stray
And autumn chill settles into the gull's reel

Where blood tides shift into sickly teal
And endless waves recoil and sway
Memories moor along the burden I feel
And autumn chill settles into the gull's reel

THE NAKED ONION

she contemplated her style
beginning to undress herself
analyzing each layer
she peeled herself
like an onion
finding like the guru
who empties his mind
the secret to herself
a microcosmic universe
for within her center
there resided no core
nucleus of onion-ness
but the nothingness that remains
when, like an onion, every layer
is stripped away
leaving only the naked poet
naked as the crucified Christ
who only then realizes
she was those layers

BEHOLD THE WIZARD

his staff
a thunderbolt

his cloak
dark sheets of hail

his foe
translucent air

a whorl of smoke
the stench of skunk

Moses,
Merlin, Gandalf

graybeards
in lightning spell craft . . .

      a recluse
      fingers his magic bone—
      mountain hermitage

FATHER

mandrake moon
in a rustling forest
a strange bird calls . . .

Father never complained of the poison mushrooms, simply moved on to the shrooms. He filled the castle with answers, cracked outrageous mysteries.

In upstairs rooms children screamed of demons in the dark. But Father hustled up those stony steps, forded impossible passes, forged by monsters who'd eat you alive like a spreading cancer.

All fathers are mortal, risk themselves on ladders, asses full of polyps.

Father always told us who we are depends on whether we break the rules like matchsticks or wild horses. We always almost listened.

STATUS QUO

Surfing the Net, one search leads to another until I'm staring at images of nude and semi-nude women and men, mostly women, protesting war, rape, Sharia, fur, meat, Trump, Burberry, body image, and even just the unnaturalness of clothing. I scroll down and pause at a single image: a nude woman in the desert, with "I destroy the family" written in black across her skin. It reminds me of a Thanksgiving from my past, when my father, a retired minister, for no apparent reason told me, "You're trying to destroy the family." I guess destroying the family is something single women do once they move beyond their youth but remain childless. The accusation left me speechless.

a cactus
fallen out of bloom—
snakeskin moon

SOMBER MUSINGS

We err, so carelessly, and to such destruction.

white pines
sagging with snow
winter blues

By the time we learn better, it's often too late.

finally falling
the old barn
where the suicide hung

FLIGHT

"We don't want you to grow up crooked," I explain to the child, hoping to sway him from teasing. His face is dirty. He wears his candy smears in colors like stained glass.

a whip-poor-will peers
from a lopsided pine tree
chilly nightfall

THE HAPPY GUY

Shopping for orange dreamsicles at Dollar Tree, I found myself in the checkout aisle behind two young men, dressed like handymen. The one closest to me suddenly declared, "I love you!" to the cashier, a large, middle-aged woman with mousy hair.

"He always embarrasses me," the other guy laughed.

"Why shouldn't I say something positive?" the man defended himself before turning to me. "I love you!" he said, a sincere smile on his face.

"I love you too," I replied with a grin.

I left the store with my dreamsicles, thinking how it isn't every day that two complete strangers look each other in the eye and say, "I love you!"

a daisy's
yellow joy . . .
warbler trills

THE MEASURE

Homeless eyes scan the endless sands
as crashing waves stir ocean treasures.
Dreams, once grand, seem so cliché, so canned—
Homeless eyes scan the endless sands.
Life doesn't always go as planned,
but how do we measure our leisure, our pleasure—
The countless stars, the countless sands—
The countless waves, our countless treasures?

WHEN I AWAKE

from dark dreams in a dead woods
to fading stars burning holes through the night
singing diasporas of hope
and taste sweet sunlight rising in the east
and like a snail peek outside my confinement . . .

when I close the book of shadows,
quieting ghosts, and open my heart
driven to and from abstraction
tossed on waves unseen
over fishes, under bridges, through the magic hour . . .

when at the sound of silver trumpets I awake
slip through the vortex of screaming silence
and pilgrimage to surreptitious place
where spirit never burns and gardens ever bloom . . .

when I awake . . .
tongues of flame
and word made flesh

WHERE THE BUTTERFLY ROAMS

THE APOCALYPSE

"All go unto one place; all are of the dust, and all turn to dust again."
Ecclesiastes 3:20

The pride of life fails
Elijah disappears on the breeze
Death arrives like an earthquake
Voices crack like sand paper
Riddle full with grit
Bones break like peanut brittle

Bullets thud into bull's-eyes
Thick torsos of meat
Marring shamrock
Anchor or nude girlie tattoos
Bodies fizzle out with a hiss

Fingers un-grip that held on for so long
Releasing life
The bitten-into poisoned apple
A pulse
A whisper
The ghost

The apocalypse finishes all
Ships crash into harbors
Leaking oil like blood
Passengers wail
Arms raised in supplication to their god

The pride of life fails
The blush of health pales
We read it in the tea leaves
Sighing beside the windowpane

THE SECOND COMING

Political smut overcasts the sky
the dust bowl
rushing across the plains
while the white pines
whip with the wind—
a pathetic fallacy.

Lobbyists hustle Washington,
full of passionate intensity,
tiptoeing into negative capability,
the futility quivering.

The world's a troll that's turned to stone.
The poem's a lie,
a Disco Word Orgy
that moons the sky
now kingdom come.

Read me! Read me!
it cries. Stanzas
stack up pig pile
like skyscrapers
then tumble
down to dust.

Deserts fill with dragons. Witches
ride their little brooms
like Halloween in July. Oceans wail.
Tectonic plates shift. Planets
line up like skid row inmates for lunch.

The sun shies away with wounded pride,
and the gay men green cheese grin.

Crows grow old beneath their feather boas,
waiting for the beast.

Turning, turning,
the world keeps turning,
waiting for the beast,
hunched on his haunches like Pan—
hairy, breasted, phallused—
Hecate.

THE ESCHATOLOGIST

After the apocalypse, the man who awaited Christ
Combs through ruined Armageddon, a ghost town,
Seeking survivors, finding mostly rubble, bodies diced.

Now, naked to the heavens, a demented heist—
After the apocalypse, the man who awaited Christ—
The giver and the gifted, blessed twice?

A soldier in death's rapture, yet he's lost his crown—
After the apocalypse, the man who awaited Christ
combs through wasted Armageddon—a ghost town.

THE END

Some days the magic dims.
There seems to be no grand analogies.
Why bother poking your head
out the Pagani in pink lipstick?
The plural for hippopotamus is hippopotami,
yet can they sing?

a la piffin
a la paffin
a la po pe puffin
& a rin-tin-tin

Darkness covers the land.
Lost in a labyrinth,
we arrive at a zugzwang . . .

The stones are cold
in the halls of the damned.
Still men fall.

A final request: Please,
let us close with something glistening:

After people,
alone beneath the palm,
a calm iguana faces
the effulgent rain.

TUNDRA

my heart
is heavy with
the death of things—
frozen
with ice age chill—
wintry sheets
centuries thick—
carcasses compressed
into oily swill—
above the ooze
and mush—
decomposed and crushed—
a single mammoth tusk
protrudes . . .

Christ,
let arctic azalea
blossom on the tomb

THE EMPTY URN

how large the moons seems
sinking low on the horizon
as if weighted by all our sorrow
to ride the mountain's back
voiceless
silhouette like Quasimodo

the hump lasts only a minute
then lets go
surrendering to dusk

how strange
our twilight beginnings
and final demise
ending in the same apothecary blues
flecked with stars

we open with a flower's softness
take the rain
harden like an iceberg
then slowly melt
swallowed again by seas
returning from whence we came
ashes to ashes
dust to dust

how strange our silence
we always believe we'll go on
and yet we're never too sure

NEVER DIE

the atom has been split
fractured into infinite particles
shaken into manic froth
but you pay the price if you break the rules
whether you break them
like matchsticks or wild horses
silly goose
you should know better than to tread on mines
though they tell you it's for the glory of Allah

One horse = horse
Two + horse = horses
One goose = goose
Two + goose = geese
One moose = moose
Two + moose = meese?

do we dare get away
go out and mosh
forget quantum physics
slamdance against the walls
like the smashed particles at Cern
those injured withdraw
our fragments from the shrapnel
our spleens from the spears
our crumbs from the crows
maintain our pulse
and though our atoms burst
never close our eyes
never stop breathing

TWILIGHT SERENITY

twilight
serenity
settling
deep
inside
the
lobster-
man's
pith

THE WEED-FILLED PATH

What lies at the end of the weed-filled path?
Autumn has come, and the sun is missing.
Wild oats, wild grapes, or the grapes of wrath—
What lies at the end of the weed-filled path?
The end of days and all its aftermath—
Some surmise a bog with bullfrogs croaking.
What lies at the end of the weed-filled path?
Winter has come, and the moon is missing.

EPILOGUE

crimson sky—
the winding road lies
behind me

wilderness
breaks for a clearing—
silent birds

old apple tree—
gnarled branches grapple
with heaven

a spent apple
succumbs to mush—
starry twilight

TAU

sohcahtoa.
check the math;
death takes us all, eventually. some
live long and die in their vigor. others . . .

peace. rest. some
long for relief impossible
through potions and pills

though the end poses
no easy answers
no simple pi
where x-intercepts
oblique, obtuse
and yet

unflinching cosmos
billows with rainbow worlds
vividly literal beside any
parallel reality, and so,

who knows?

WHERE THE BUTTERFLY ROAMS

in silent meetings
purveyors of arcane magic
sometimes guessed
there is no escape
from rebirth, only death

bread, wine, and oil
burning incense and psalms
we struggle with the notes
divine fire forged
the cosmos where we race
toward final consummation

eternity . . .
though mountains wear away
still the streams flow
where the butterfly roams
there is no reason

the butterfly
fears neither darkness
nor the strange light
it does not suffer
the death of stars

Bibliography

Geoffrey, Parrinder, ed. *World Religions: From Ancient History to the Present*. New York: Newnes Books, 1971.

"Golem." https://en.wikipedia.org/wiki/Golem

www.ingramcontent.com/pod-product-compliance
Lightning Source LLC
LaVergne TN
LVHW021550080426
835510LV00019B/2455